Mentoring Mandate:

Making 21st Century Disciples

Stan E. DeKoven, Ph.D.

Mentoring Mandate

Stan DeKoven

Copyright 2015 © Stan DeKoven

ISBN: 978-1-61529-155-7

Vision Publishing
1115 D Street
Ramona, CA 92065
1 800 9-VISION
www.booksbyvision.com

Table of Contents

Introduction

In scripture, there are two primary illustrations of training for men and women in ministry...really three when you consider Jesus, which of course, we always should.

In the Old Testament, the Bible relates a spiritually significant story of the elder Prophet Elijah[1], whose mantle of authority and anointing was passed on to his servant, Elisha (2 Kings 2). The mantle was old and worn. It had served Elijah well. It was with him, enduring the cold lonely nights in the wilderness. He had used it to wrap himself when he prayed. The mantle was with Elijah on Mt. Carmel as he confronted a wicked king and backslidden Israel and called down fire from heaven.

For years, Elisha shadowed Elijah. They ate together. They traveled together. They prayed together. Elisha witnessed the mighty manifestation of God's power as Elijah ministered in supernatural power and authority.

Years later, when he and Elisha stood at the Jordan River, Elijah took the mantle in his hands and struck the river. The waters parted, and they walked together across the river on dry ground. When Elijah's ministry ended and the time came for him to go to the Father, he looked down upon Elisha from the fiery chariot and, in that final fleeting moment, the mantle fell from his shoulders and landed at Elisha's feet. Elisha, with one final glimpse and a heartfelt cry, "My father, my father – the chariots and horsemen of Israel," was parted from his beloved father in the faith.

In great anguish, Elisha tore his clothes, ran to where Elijah's mantle had fallen on the ground, and picked it up. He held it in his hands, this symbol of the prophetic anointing of God's Spirit that had rested upon Elijah. When Elisha took up that mantle, it was

---

[1] I am grateful to Dr. Patricia Hulsey for her original ideas on this section, and the Morris Cerullo School of Ministry manual.

based upon the prophetic word that he indeed would receive from Elisha a double-portion of his dynamic ministry.

From the day that mantle passed into his hands, Elisha ministered in a double-portion anointing.

Elisha wrapped the mantle together as he had seen Elijah do and walked to the banks of the Jordan River. The mantle was only a symbol. He knew that his title as Elijah's successor, and the mantle he wore and all it symbolized would be in vain unless the same power and anointing of God's Spirit that was upon Elijah rested upon him.

As Elisha struck the mantle upon the waters, he cried out, "*Where is the Lord God of Elijah?*" and God responded in a demonstration of his power by parting the Jordan River just as he had done for Elijah. In the distance, fifty sons of the prophets saw the demonstration of God's power and declared, "The Spirit of Elijah rests on Elisha!"

How many of us have prayed for a double portion. Perhaps you have been prayed for by someone guaranteeing you would receive it, only to be disappointed. Well, we must remember that only Elisha received a double portion. No other incident like this is seen or repeated in scripture, as there was only one parting of the Red Sea, one donkey speaking to a prophet, one Daniel in the lion's den, etc. You may never receive a double portion of another man or woman of God's anointing or gifting, but you can grow and mature in your own, just as Timothy did under Paul's tutelage.

The Jesus Model

As previously mentioned, who can (or should) forget Jesus? Jesus had two primary goals for his ministry; the cross and discipling the next generation once they were empowered by Holy Spirit. In Mark 3: 13-15 we read;

> "And he went up to the mountain and summoned those whom he himself wanted, and they came to

him. And he appointed twelve that they might be with him, and that he might send them out to preach, and to have authority to cast out the demons."

Jesus began his ministry preaching the Kingdom of God and performing miracles. Many followed him, including the twelve he eventually called. In prayer to the Father, Jesus first called the men, the ones he selected from the many who were following him. The called were then in a position to choose. These two principles are still true today.

For the person wanting to be chosen (to be mentored or a student) must be willing, demonstrated by faithful following, to be called. No doubt, Jesus, in consultation with the Father, did the calling. But also note, that those called had the option to refuse; only the willing and able (in this case, middle class small business owners with the ability to follow, contribute and with time to serve) could follow. He appointed them, first to be with him, as relationship is essential in discipleship/mentoring. Then he prepared them to preach with authority, just as Jesus did, and to minister in the power of Holy Spirit as Jesus did. The book of Acts tells the tale of Jesus' effectiveness.

Paul and Timothy

In an even more profound way, Paul had a young man named Timothy who he adopted as a son, taught him the ways of a man of God, and encouraged and promoted him into leadership in Ephesus and beyond. They had a unique father/son relationship, as seen in Paul's writings to Timothy in the epistles titled after him. Paul found Timothy a faithful young man, able to teach others, which he encouraged him to continue to do in his apostolic/pastoral ministry (2 Timothy 2:2).

These are by far the best biblical models for mentoring or discipleship we have. They are models which can be duplicated today, enhanced by modern technology. Yes, the same power and anointing that rested upon Elijah and Elisha, and was transferred from Paul to Timothy {and then on to faithful others} has been delegated to us. The same mandate to equip and disciple men and women to maturity is ours. This is the mantle of the anointing passed from the hands of Jesus into our hands when he ascended to his Father. Thus, the questions to ask every young man or woman wanting to serve the Lord include:

- Are you ready to pick up the mantle of God's anointing and strike it upon the waters of your life?
- Are you ready to prepare the next generation of leaders to walk into the fulfillment of God's promises and purposes?
- Are you ready to serve your generation by meeting the needs of the world- proclaiming the Word, healing the sick, and bringing a harvest of souls?

If so, then you are ready to rise up in the spirit and power of Elijah, train a multitude of Elisha's, and transfer to them the teaching of Christ, as Paul did to Timothy and Timothy to others who were then faithful to teach others.

The Key Purpose

The purpose of this book is to help men and women to mentor or coach effectively, professionally, and thoroughly, men and women with a call of God on their lives. This function, of mentoring and training for the next generation has been the passion of this author and the team of the International Training College Internship Program, in conjunction with Vision International University. Its divine mission, our biblical strategy for reproduction, and mentoring guidelines are presented here, with a hope that other schools, pastors and leaders will take the principles and run with them to even greater success. This book also provides as a model the practical guidelines for establishing a Mentor Center, information on the usage of and importance of conservative charismatic curriculum, and administrative resources to assist the local church to develop an on line or off line mentoring center.

For those who are joining the International Training College Mentoring Program,[2] included with this book will be additional Mentoring Materials, which includes our core course teachings; the life transforming materials developed by Dr. Ken Chant and Dr. Stan DeKoven and other dynamic leaders, and other resources found on our patented Bible College in a Box CD. The spiritual truths that have impacted hundreds of thousands around the world and birthed some of the greatest ministries in existence today are yours to prepare your men and women for generational ministry. A wealth of supplemental training materials is also included to assist you in seizing the mantle of God's anointing as it passes into your hands.

As you become more familiar with the mentoring ministry, you can be easily overwhelmed with the amount of content and the responsibility of mentoring and coaching the next generation of leaders. But please know, you can, by God's grace, teach and train, and help those future leaders God has joined to you become all God intended them to be. With your commitment to serve in your local community using the many comprehensive programs and services available, a mantle of divine authority will be passed on to you. The future is in your hands. Take up this mantle and go forth in the spirit and power of Elijah, with the wisdom and strategy of Paul.

> *"He will also go before Him in the spirit and power of Elijah, to turn the hearts of the fathers to the children, and the disobedient to the wisdom of the just, to make ready a people prepared for the Lord"*
>
> *Luke 1:17, NKJV.*

In Mutual Service,

Stan E. DeKoven, Ph.D

---

[2] For more information, see www.vision.edu

P.S. Along with this book, for new members of ITC Mentoring Center, you have been provided 1 CD (for Administration) which has all the forms, university catalog, approved promotional brochures (which you can modify with prior approval) and a DVD explaining the mentor process and ITC/Mentor Center. After reviewing this material, please take a few minutes to review the DVD and CD…it will help solidify your choice to follow Christ in mentoring the next generation for Kingdom Expansion.

Chapter 1

Mentoring Objectives

The objectives of any mentoring program are to transfer the vision of the Great Commission, motivated by the Great Commandment, to the next and future generations. This was the goal of the establishment of Vision International University and our mentoring programs. By way of illustration, here is a brief history of Vision and our Mentoring Program, called our School of Ministry.

HISTORY OF THE ITC/VISION SCHOOL OF MINISTRY

In 1974, Vision began both in Tasmania, Australia and San Diego, California. Dr. Ken Chant founded Vision Bible College in Launceston, Tasmania. Simultaneously, Dr. Joseph Bohac and Dr. Stan DeKoven began Logos Institute, a local church training program in practical ministry and counseling.

By 1977, Dr. Chant moved his school to Sydney, Australia, joining Dr. Allan Langstaff. While Dr. DeKoven pursued his graduate studies; Logos Institute continued as a counseling ministry.

In 1980 Dr. Chant moved to St. Paul, Minnesota and established his program there. Dr. DeKoven returned to San Diego, earned his doctorate in Psychology, and continued to expand the Logos program. Simultaneously, Dr. Randy Gurley, now Chairman of Vision's Board of Regents, began his Bible College teaching ministry, which eventually merged with Vision.

Dr. Chant, in response to a strong leading from the Lord, brought his outstanding Bible College to San Diego, California, where Vision Bible College was incorporated as a non-profit ministry in 1985.

By 1987, Dr. DeKoven and Dr. Chant had established a full-time, short-term campus and eventually merged their hearts and visions. The network of affiliated resource centers, the desire of Dr. DeKoven's heart, began to be established and has grown as is described hereafter.

Greater Growth

A pivotal year for Vision was 1990 when Dr. Chant, in obedience to the Lord, returned to his native Australia. Prior to his leaving, Vision Bible College, under Dr. DeKoven's direction, had expanded to its present University status. A headquarters site was obtained in the beautiful community of Ramona, California, where the present headquarters continues to be based, along with a counseling and education center. Religious Exemption to grant degrees by the Bureau of Private Post-Secondary Education (BPPE) in the State of California was awarded.

Throughout the 1990s, staff and faculty were added to the institution, mostly volunteers, who contributed to curriculum development and student support. The institution expanded rapidly internationally, as the mission of the institution was, and has remained, to provide education and training to religious leadership where such opportunities are either financially problematic or unavailable. In this sense, Vision International University was much more a movement than an institution.

In 1998 Vision began dialog with the Transnational Association of Christian Colleges and Schools (TRACS) concerning accreditation. Initially, this looked to be an excellent agency to work with toward our goal. Vision voluntarily withdrew from the process of pursuing TRACS after recognizing that in order to meet the standards demanded by the association, the delivery method and mission of the organization would have to be significantly altered. The preparation leading to dialog with TRACS, however, produced positive results in curriculum upgrades and development, streamlining of policies and procedures, and strategic planning.

During this time VIU also explored some non-USDE approved accrediting agencies, but determined that for integrity's sake we should not pursue that direction for our distance University.

The institution continued to grow into the 2000s as international expansion continued and new partners, faculty, and staff were added. By the year 2000, Vision programs were implemented in 116 nations. However, the administrative structure, organizational structure, and communication channels were still very informal. The need for new leadership, staff, and technology was apparent.

In 2004, a stronger distinction began to be drawn between international operations and programs in the United States. Following the accreditation of Vision International College Australia, a new model for Vision International University was adopted. Delivery of education at local sites was converted to Direct Distance Education for students, though they may convene for mutual support at a local center. VIU now offers its program either by direct distance correspondence, seminar based or online.

Also in 2004, Vision International University began working toward State Approval by the California Bureau of Private Post-Secondary Education (now Bureau of Private Post-Secondary Education, 2010). Working with educational consultants, the institution made many significant improvements, policy changes, and curricular adaptations in the application process, which was a much needed small-scale self-study that allowed the institution to rethink its methods and further improve its operations.

During this time, the institution also had a site visit with the Association for Biblical Higher Education (ABHE). Dialog with the association concluded that the best option for Vision International University was to pursue accreditation with the Distance Education and Training Council, as the institution's programs were entirely distance in nature. It was recommended that Vision International University apply for affiliate membership with the ABHE, which was awarded in the summer of 2006.

As restructuring continued, it was apparent that new distinctions needed to be made in programs that were offered. In 2005, the ministry restructured, organizing several different ministries under the International Training and Education Network, Inc. ITEN and the International Training College is a separate and autonomous corporation distinct from VIU, and educational programs are religious exempt, and are non-governmentally accredited by the International Association of Bible Colleges and Seminaries.

Vision International University has been established as the sole program of Vision International Education Services, Inc. Major technological advances were achieved in 2006 including the automation of several operational processes, record keeping, and web-based marketing and delivery of curriculum. The year 2006 also marked the addition of new faculty, revised curriculum, the addition of the Institute for Theological Studies courses, and the organization of new administrative decision-making committees.

Further in 2006, major restructuring continued as accreditation became a more realistic goal. Temporary State Approval was awarded to Vision International University in June 2006. (Permanent State Approval was granted April 4, 2007.) The approval was for entirely new degree programs, designed only for distance education students. Vision International University continues to pursue accreditation with a national accrediting agency, which continues to the present time.

Chapter 2

The Mentor Center

The concept of a mentor center has been around for a long time. Local church based training is *the* biblical model for education. However, how education and training is delivered in and through the local church has changed, and in many ways for the better. Technology has helped us to deliver content to the local student, via direct correspondence or online. However, this does not replace the vital importance of local church accountability, mentoring and pastoral input for true discipleship to occur. The programs of any mentor center must provide the systems and content to prepare men and women for effective service in the local church and beyond, without compromising the importance of local leadership input.

THE BIBLICAL PHILOSOPHY

Acts 19:1-20 records the ministry of Apostle Paul in the city of Ephesus. When Paul first arrived in Ephesus, he sought out disciples who had accepted the Gospel and became followers of Jesus, but needed further training in order to minister effectively in their city (Acts 19:1). When opposition to the Gospel arose from traditional leaders, Paul established a training center for disciples at Ephesus:

> *"But when some were hardened and did not believe, but spoke evil of the Way before the multitude, he departed from them and withdrew the disciples, reasoning daily in the school of Tyrannus" (Acts 19:9).*

The ITC/Vision Mentoring Center, as with all biblically based mentoring ministries, is modeled after the biblical example of Antioch and Ephesus, where informal and semi-formal schools were established which trained and equipped believers for the work of the ministry. From my perspective, the best model is that of the church in Ephesus. Their purpose was to spread the Gospel geographically (throughout all Asia) and culturally (to both Jews and Gentiles). Some of these disciples may have been businessmen or farmers, but the Ephesus school did not train them in these professions. It trained them to be reproductive disciples, whether they worked in the market place or as full-time pastors in the local church.

The training center did not replace the church. Believers continued to meet in synagogues, churches, and homes. The Ephesus school was an extension of the local church.

The city of Ephesus, which Paul selected as the location for his school, was a busy trading port. It was also a center for tourism and headquarters for the cult of the false goddess Diana. All of these factors resulted in many people living in and visiting the city of Ephesus. Reaching the large population of Ephesus with the Gospel provided great opportunity for training students. Not only could the Gospel be preached to the masses who lived in the city, but there was opportunity to reach thousands who visited the city as tourists or on business. When these visitors who accepted the Gospel went home, they returned to hundreds of other cities and villages to spread the Gospel.

Because Ephesus was the center of the cult of the false goddess Diana, it provided opportunities for training in how to deal with demon possession and occult practices. If students could learn to deal with the demonic forces at work in this evil city, they would certainly be able to minister in other locations of lesser satanic influence.

Paul did not remove disciples from their native environment to receive training. He trained them in an environment which was natural to them. They remained in their own community and learned in their own language. This is the same vision of The Mentor Center.

Paul taught the believers in Ephesus through experience. The first thing he did was lead them into a new spiritual experience; the baptism of the Holy Spirit (Acts 19:2-8). Through the demonstration of God's power in his own life, Paul taught them by example. They witnessed many great miracles done in the name of the Lord (Acts 19:11-12). Those who were not true followers of Jesus were exposed and repented (Acts 19:13-17) and new converts were won to the Lord Jesus Christ (Acts 19:17-20).

The center Paul established offered short-term training with the purpose of multiplying disciples who would spread the Gospel message:

> *"But when some were hardened and did not believe, but spoke evil of the Way before the multitude, he departed from them and withdrew the disciples, reasoning daily in the school of Tyrannus. And this continued for two years, so that all who dwelt in Asia heard the word of the Lord Jesus, both Jews and Greeks." (Acts 19:9-10)*

This center knew no cultural barriers. Students ministered to both Jews and Gentiles (other non-Jewish nations of the world). The school had no geographic boundaries. The students not only ministered in their own city of Ephesus, they reached the entire continent of Asia "*…so that all they which dwelt in Asia heard the word of the Lord Jesus, both Jews and Greeks…So mightily grew the word of God and prevailed*" (Acts 19:10 and 20).

The school at Ephesus trained believers to be effective ministers of the Gospel and these disciples multiplied spiritually to reach all of Asia with the Word of God. Paul also multiplied his own ministry by establishing such a center.

In Acts 19:23-41 and 20:1, we learn that the production and sale of occult objects, books, etc., was big business at Ephesus. When people repented from sin and followed the way of the Gospel, they no longer purchased these items used in the worship of false gods.

They also burned items previously purchased. The merchants who made their living from the sale of these items became very angry, a riot resulted, and in the end, Paul had to leave the city.

However when Paul departed, he left something very important behind at Ephesus. He left a group of trained disciples to carry on the work of the Gospel. He left an established training center which continued the multiplication process when he could no longer remain in the city.

The need for similar training centers still exists today. As nations experience political change, many missionaries are forced to leave countries where they have ministered. This is why mentoring in a systematic fashion is so important.

As spiritual mentor with the wisdom of Paul, you will train men and women to not only be dynamic followers of Jesus, but also equip them to raise up other Timothy's so that this powerful mantle of spiritual anointing can continue to multiply around the world.

For more on the Ephesus model, see Dr. DeKoven's book, Supernatural Architecture, www.booksbyvision.com.

Chapter 3

5 C's Philosophy of Leadership Development[3]

An effective leader possesses:
- Calling
- Character
- Competence

All three elements are found in the description of King David in Psalm 78. Just as a stool has three legs, there are three foundations of effective leadership; calling, character and competence. However, though these three characteristics are foundation stones to effective leadership, there remains two elements missing in our model: Christ and Community, which come from Christ's teaching in Mathew 22:35-40.

Christ

For healthy leaders to be developed in our churches, Christ must come first, for true leadership is not possible without Christ first! Without Christ first in the life of the leader, he will never function fully in the community of faith (Titus 3:3). Finally, man's competencies are useless apart from Christ. Without Christ first, the leader is capable of nothing of any value in God's eyes (John 15:5). It is the only way to true Christian leadership. Jesus' leadership came from His union with His Father. In the relationship between Jesus and His Father, we are going to find a parallel to what our own relationship with God can be. {John 6:56-57} Jesus' leadership entirely came from His union through living by His Father's life, revealing His Father to the world, so we, through living by means of Jesus' indwelling life, will express His life and being to the world. As Paul testified:

---

[3] The author is grateful to the seminal work of Dr. Malcolm Weber on these five keys to healthy leaders.

"...God...was pleased to reveal his Son in me..." (Galatians 1:15-16). This is the simple nature of the Christian life: union with Jesus, and living by means of His indwelling life. Thus, this is the source of Christian leadership, and Jesus' disciples led out of their fellowship with Him (Acts 4:13).

Community

The Christian life is personal union and fellowship with Jesus (John 17:3). Church life is knowing God together. Together the community of believer's can experience God in His fullness. (1 Cor. 12:12-14) Spiritual maturity is a corporate experience, not just an individual one. (John 13:34-35) In the life of the community, as we love and serve one another, the daily realities of our own walks with Jesus are expressed in our relationships with one another. Thus, Christian unity is not a unity of structure, but of fellowship. Christian fellowship is a heart to heart, "deep calls to deep," intimate spiritual communion. Church life is both a foretaste and a beginning of everlasting life.

Leaders, too, need healthy communities around them, communities that will uphold and strengthen them, communities with loving accountability, trust, and unconditional acceptance, communities that will challenge them to authenticity. In these "safe environments," people have the freedom to be honest and to grow within boundaries framed by shared values and common goals. Such healthy organizational communities nurture character. Healthy community forms the context in which individual callings and responsibilities are expressed in order to fulfill the community's corporate purpose.

The leader develops in community (Ephesians 4:13-16). In reality, we only really mature and grow as Christians in the context of community. Further, the leader leads in the context of community (Romans 12; 4-8; 1 Corinthians 12-27). Effective Christian leaders must lead in a context of community, not as tough "ministry islands" off by themselves.

20

Character

No leader will be perfect- other than the Lord Jesus. However, leaders reflect God Himself to men; they must be of the highest character. The minister's shortcomings simply cannot be concealed. He who is required by the necessity of his position to speak the highest things is compelled by the same necessity to exemplify the highest things. *Gregory the Great (540-604)*

Prayer, meditation, and temptation make a minister. *Martin Luther (1483-1546)* People are not only motivated to follow by the leader's captivating vision or by his compelling communication skills, but also by their sense of the leader's desire to serve, his high integrity and consistency. Character is a "non-negotiable" requirement. In fact, **Training Fails When Character is Not Developed**. Scholastic accomplishment neither makes nor breaks a missionary. It is but one factor in the complex of influences which have formed the man himself.

> ▶ There are several lists in the New Testament of the specific character qualities of a godly leader:
>   - Galatians 5:22-23
>   - 2 Peter 1:5-8

There are 3 essential elements in developing healthy character: **discipline, proving and accountability**

At the heart of character lies discipline {1 Corinthians 9:24-27; Proverbs 25:28} When discipline matures, he is then permitted by God to give discipline to others. He has become a leader.

True character is formed in the context of Christ and Community in these 3 stages:

1. First the emerging leader submits to discipline.
2. Then, in that context, internal discipline is built. This is self-discipline, self-control.
3. Once internal discipline is in place, God permits him, and man trusts him, to lead others.

This order cannot be reversed and none of the steps can be skipped. Internal discipline must be in place in the leader before he can effectively lead others.

A leader does not become one overnight. He must be tested first. (1 Timothy 3:10) He must undergo the preparations of God.

This goes against our culture, which wants instant success. We want to start at "the top," but that is not the way of God. These are the unchanging ways of God: preparation and proving precede leadership:

- ▶ Moses spent 40 years in the wilderness before he was released as a leader.
- ▶ Joseph spent years in prison before he ruled Egypt
- ▶ David lived in the wilderness for years before he was trusted to rule Israel
- ▶ John the Baptist grew up in the wilderness, spending almost 30 years in preparation before he was finally commissioned as an apostle.
- ▶ Jesus' disciples were all personally prepared and proven by Jesus before He entrusted them with the leadership of His church.
- ▶ Paul underwent extensive preparation before he was finally commissioned as an apostle.
- ▶ Jesus' disciples were all personally prepared and proven by Jesus before he entrusted them with the leadership of His church.
- ▶ The Lord Jesus Himself "Increased in wisdom and stature, and in favor with God and man" (Luke 2:52), and learned obedience from what he suffered" (Hebrews 5:8)

Thus, Paul instructs us that a novice should not be given primary leadership responsibility. Emerging leaders must be given time to learn, to be proven, to learn discipline and to be broken, in order for character to be formed.

The emerging leader must learn to choose accountability. The word means being answerable for your actions. People think of Paul as an independent ministry, accountable to no one but God. But Paul was sent out by the church at Antioch (Acts 13:3) and he remained accountable to that spiritual community throughout his ministry (Acts 14:26-28; 15:2-3, 35-40; 18:22-23) Paul willingly made himself accountable to the leaders of the church at Jerusalem, from whom the gospel had initially come (Acts 21:17-26; cf. Gal.2:2). Accountability is central to character and to effective leadership.

Healthy leaders will be accountable ones! A top leader who does not presently have a relationship of accountability built into the system of his community should seek an outside relationship of accountability. To help define what character is, we should also examine what it is not:

1. Character is not just what a person will ideally be in the future. Character is what a person is at this present time.
2. It is not only how a person acts. It also includes a person's inner thoughts, motives and attitudes.
3. Does not appear without pressure.
4. Character is not only that which other people see on the external. It is what other people do not see.
5. Character is not limited to having wisdom to comment on the behaviors of others.
6. Is not limited to relationships between Christians.
7. Is not limited to a person's relationship with his spiritual family.

To a man of character, God can entrust a calling.

Calling

A leader must have a calling and a vision from God or else he would be wise not to lead (James 3:1). There is no substitute for the divine call in the leader's life. Strong calling must not be disconnected from a deep surrender to and relationship with Christ. Christ comes first!

A true calling comes from God. Then it becomes the leader's own vision; something he can share passionately with others. In addition, the calling must be submitted to community. Today, man-appointed leaders look upon spiritual leadership as a profession or a career. They are more concerned with the medical benefits or retirement accounts that come with the "job" than they are for the sheep of God. They are the "hired hands" (John 10:12-13).

True leadership will be appointed by God. Leaders will be aware of the call of God on their lives. They may fight or deny the call for a while, but they will still know God has called them

One's individual calling will be the result of a very complex interaction between the following elements in a leader's life:

- Personality
- Culture
- Gender
- Age
- Physical condition
- Leader/manager orientation
- Genes
- Life expectations
- Relationships
- Role models
- Mentors
- Family heritage
- Current family
- Spiritual gifts
- Motivational gifts
- Ministry gifts
- Formal education
- Training experiences

Thus, there are not only 5 callings (e.g., Ephesians 4) but an almost infinite number of callings that match each individual perfectly in the purposes of God. A divine calling to lead establishes the leader's purpose, passion and commission. Without a clear understanding of his purpose, the leader will not accomplish much. Leaders must have a clear purpose for their leadership and this purpose must be established by God. Having a clear understanding of his calling will allow the leader to focus and be more effective (e.g., Exodus 18:13-26; 2 Corinthians 10:13-18).

The way is frequently hard (Acts 14:22); only the truly committed will make it. Leadership is risky work. Only those who can passionately communicate the exciting possibilities of the future will be able to persuade others to follow them down a frequently difficult path. People need strong visionary leadership to help them start moving and to keep on moving. People sacrifice for passionate vision.

In the leader's life, there will be a specific time of divine commission when he is set apart for the work to which God has called him. This commission was given by the Holy Spirit Acts 13:4; cf. Matthew 9:38; 1 Corinthians 1:1; Galatians 1:1; Deuteronomy 31:14) in the context of the authority structure of the church ("they placed their hands on them and sent them off", Acts 13:3; cf. Acts 6:3-6)

Thus, the calling comes from God and is then confirmed by the community. Remember this; authority does not come from gifting; it comes from the commission. As you are faithful in what He gives you to do, God might expand your field of ministry (Luke 16:10). Paul faithfully taught for years before receiving his apostolic commission.

Competency

Many Christian leaders fail due to a lack of competency. They have a good knowledge of the Bible, but they have never learned how to lead people or manage the practical aspects of an organization. Other leaders do have good strategic and technical abilities to lead, but they lack sound biblical knowledge. They are able to build a large, and apparently successful church or ministry but they lead it into spiritual error. Again, the issue is inadequate competencies (2 Timothy 3:14-17). Paul told Timothy to choose elders who had some basic organizational competencies (1 Timothy 3:4-5). This was in contrast to the false leaders at Ephesus who did not know what they were doing (1 Timothy 1:7). Thus, the leader must "know how" to do it. A vast majority of Pastors do not believe they have the "Gift of Leadership".

A future leader also needs experience in ministry before he is commissioned. His spiritual community is the safe context in which he should "practice" as he grows as an emerging leader. As the leader matures he will experience changes in task and responsibilities. There are many kinds of competencies that are necessary for leaders to have. Essentially, the individual's calling defines his necessary competencies. Competence is the last part of our model of a healthy leader. It is absolutely necessary that a leader have strong competencies.

Chapter 4

Defining Mission

The mission is ultimately the purpose for which a ministry exists. For example, for Vision International University our mission is to effectively educate and train men and women called to Christian service by means of distance education. The academic model shall be biblically based Christian higher education (undergraduate through graduate), for preparing Christian pastors, missionaries, church leaders, educators and other professionals for leadership in various fields of Christian service. This mission is to be accomplished through a Christ-centered distance education curriculum, of academic excellence, intellectual inquiry, spiritual and moral integrity, and practical experience.

Values or Principles

For a ministry to be effective, it must be committed to certain values or biblical principles. Again, by way of example, for Vision International University and our International Training College Mentoring ministry we espouse to:

- An identity as a Christian institution of higher education, serving qualified applicants without sectarian discrimination.
- A firm biblical emphasis, both in curriculum and in principles for praxis, based upon acceptance of the authority of the scriptures.
- A competent, theologically diverse faculty committed to a quality academic program.
- A comprehensive educational philosophy, the practices of which are supported by rigorous empirical research.
- A sense of community that fosters positive relationships among faculty and students of diverse backgrounds.

- A learning environment supportive of the local church.
- A commitment to a progressive approach in addressing the technological nature of our changing society.

Statement of Faith

This leads us, and any ministry, to an affirmation of a statement of faith, which further defines the principles by which we live and serve. For example, we state that the curriculum of Vision attempts to maintain a non-dogmatic perspective, allowing students to study a wide variety of theological issues to formulate their own beliefs in an academic context. Vision maintains a strong emphasis on church planting, community service, and Christian character development.

The inter-denominational, non-sectarian institution of the Vision International University offer ministry training and theological education to students from a wide variety of faith backgrounds. Vision International began in Australia in 1974 as a Pentecostal-Charismatic institution without specific denominational affiliation. Vision now cooperates with many Christian denominations and ministerial fellowships to provide a primarily biblical education to both students preparing for vocational ministry and those who seek a stronger theological foundation for the ministerial context in which they find themselves. Vision welcomes students from any denominational background.

This is not intended to be a comprehensive statement of faith, but rather a guide to the doctrinal boundaries within which Vision functions. Those who share our spiritual identity will be generally familiar with the following terms, and will be able to fill in what is lacking. Local communities are encouraged, as designed, to develop a statement of faith that varies on minor points of doctrine, from Vision's.

We affirm the following:

- That the Bible is the Word of God, given and preserved for all generations. We believe it is accurate in all that it ultimately affirms, and is the authoritative standard by which we determine beliefs and conduct.
- That God exists as three persons: The Father, Jesus Christ His only Son our Lord, who offers saving grace to all, and the Holy Spirit who empowers men and women for service, and sanctifies them for God's purpose.
- That nothing can replace the importance of the local church, which is the body of Christ on earth, in the program of God.
- That entrance into the church is through the "new birth", which is brought about by genuine repentance of sin, confession of faith in Christ as Savior, and surrender to him as Lord.
- That membership in the church is signified by joyful participation in its worship, fellowship, sacraments, witness, and by acceptance of its discipline.
- That the presence and use of the charismata is essential in the local church and in Christian ministry.
- That the victorious Christian life is built upon a proper understanding and exercise of the spiritual authority conveyed to the believer by the gift of righteousness.
- In the resurrection of the dead at Christ's return, in the certainty of God's judgment, and in the inescapable result of that judgment as foretold in the scriptures for the just and the unjust.

Our Role:

Our role at Vision is to bring theological education and ministerial training to people who are unable or unwilling to attend a centralized higher education institution.

But more profoundly, while we admire and endorse the efforts of traditional Bible Colleges and Seminaries, we are deeply committed to the concept of training people within the supervision of their own local church, and to the provision of excellent teaching material and study options for Christians everywhere. We treat the entire local church environment as part of our educational activity: its worship, its witness, its fellowship, its teaching; its ministry – are all reckoned to be part of the training process of equipping men and women to serve Christ.

- Our function is simply to add a theological and academic resource that few churches can viably provide, while leaving the practical training in ministry to the local pastor.
- Underlying the way in which we present our materials, and the kinds of assessment we employ, there is an educational philosophy based upon the following principles –

  - Christian education must stand upon a strong theological foundation (cp. the injunctions and warnings about "sound doctrine" in 1 Timothy 1:10; 4:13; 2 Timothy 4:3; 2 Peter 2:1-3; Jeremiah 6:16; 1 Corinthians 3:10-13; etc.).
  - Students must be brought to know God, not just to learn about him, and the curriculum must be consciously structured to achieve that excellent end.

The goal must be not just to impart knowledge, but rather to teach principles of sound interpretation, showing people how to do their own research, and how to apply truth to life. A final goal is the ultimate activation of men and women into effective Christian service, in any environment to which he or she may be called to minister.

Chapter 5

The Strategy of Reproduction[4]

The Gospel is to be preached to every nation. Can it be done in this generation? Only if the laity is trained to spread the Gospel message. When we speak of "laity" or "layperson" we are referring to men and women who are not professional ministers. They compose 99 percent of the church population. This is the largely untapped potential that The ITC Mentoring Manual must reach and train if we are to fulfill the Great Commission.

Rather than separate the clergy (professional ministers) from the laity, we much help each born-again believer realize his personal responsibility in fulfilling the Great Commission. The world will never be reached with the Gospel if only the ministers are responsible for sharing the message. There are not enough professional ministers to get the job done. This is where a mentor center fills such a vital purpose: Raising up key leaders who can train others to fulfill the divine mandate.

> *"And he Himself gave some to be apostles, some prophets, some evangelists, and some pastors and teachers, for the equipping of the saints for the work of ministry, for the edifying of the body of Christ, till we all come to the unity of the faith and of the knowledge of the Son of God, to a perfect man, to the measure of the stature of the fullness of Christ"*
>
> *Ephesians 4:11-13, KJV.*

---

[4] For more on this, see Dr. DeKoven's book 7 Reasons Every Local Church Should be a Ministry Training Center by Vision Publishing, www.booksbyvision.com.

THE EARLY CHURCH

Involvement of the laity was one of the keys to growth in the early Church. In Acts 8:1 we read that the persecution of Christians resulted in their scattering throughout Judea and Samaria.

Church leaders remained in Jerusalem and we find, *"...they that were scattered abroad went everywhere preaching the word"* (Acts 8:4).

Not only the leadership, but also the laity who were scattered, fulfilled an important role in spreading the Gospel message.

From the beginning, the spreading, of the Gospel was a lay movement. Men like Peter and John were untrained fishermen. The majority of ministry and missionary activity in the early Church was accomplished by non-professionals, ordinary men and women involved in secular work as occupations.

When Saul tried to destroy the early Church, the Bible records that he entered into homes as well as churches because he recognized that eliminating only churches and professional ministers would not stop the spread of the Gospel. Each layperson was a reproducing Christian and each home was a center of prayer and evangelism (Acts 8:3).

WE CAN REACH THE WORLD IN THIS GENERATION

If we are to reach the world with the Gospel message and stop the advance of the enemy, the clergy and laity must join forces. Believers are not just fragments of the Church scattered throughout the community who come together for worship, instruction, and Christian fellowship. In daily work and living they are representatives of the Kingdom of God who can reach people who will never enter a church or attend a religious meeting.

In the early Church, the spread of the Gospel was not left to the full-time pastors, prophets, evangelists, and teachers. Every New Testament believer was spiritually reproductive. If we are to reach the world with the Gospel, we must return to this strategy of the early Church. Both leaders and laymen must share the responsibility for spiritual reproduction. The growth in world population requires a return to the New Testament plan of ministry by each member of the Body of Christ. We cannot reach the world through token efforts and halfhearted dedication.

The command given by Jesus to believers is to "go" into all the world with the Gospel message. You do not have to wait for the command to go because it already has been given. In relation to the spread of the Gospel, the command is to go and watch for the stops, not stop and wait for the go.

TRAINING FAITHFUL MEN

Paul told Timothy to select faithful men and commit to them the things he had been taught. These faithful men were to have the ability to teach others. Through this organized plan of training the laity, the Gospel would spread throughout the world.

It is the selection of these faithful men and women that is the key to effective training of the laity. The world takes talented people and attempts to give them character. They focus on creating professionals. God said to take faithful men of character and He will empower them with talents and abilities to be spiritually effective.

By following the plan given in 2 Timothy 2:2, the Church can experience tremendous growth:

> *And the things that thou hast heard of me among many witnesses, the same commit thou to faithful men, who shall be able to teach others also.*

Jesus entrusted the laity with major responsibilities of the Gospel cause. Taking fishermen from their boats, He made them into fishers of men. He believed that ordinary people could become extraordinary when empowered by the Holy Spirit. This is the vision of The ITC

The purpose of a mentor center is to spread the vision of training the laity, every born-again believer, throughout the world. It is God's methodology of multiplication. It is to the laity that the Institute is geared and to the reproductive process of 2 Timothy 2:2 that we are committed.

THE HOLY SPIRIT ENABLES MULTIPLICATION

In a final message to His disciples, Jesus said:

> *"But you shall receive power when the Holy Spirit has come upon you; and you shall be witnesses to Me in Jerusalem, and in all Judea and Samaria, and to the end of the earth." (Acts 1:8)*

The power of the Holy Spirit enables multiplication. The gifts of the Holy Spirit equip believers for multiplication. The fruit of the Holy Spirit causes reproduction. The Bible speaks of four types of church growth or multiplication empowered by the Holy Spirit:

GEOGRAPHPICAL GROWTH:

Geographic growth was mandated by the Lord Jesus in Acts 1:8 where He indicated the Gospel would multiply to Jerusalem, Judea, Samaria, and to the ends of the earth.

NUMERIC GROWTH:

The Church would experience numeric growth as it grew geographically. Numeric growth of the first Church is recorded in the book of Acts. For examples, the Church had increased from 12 to 120 in Acts 1:15, to 3,000 in Acts 2:41; and to 5,000 in Acts 4:4.

ETHINC GROWTH:

The early Church experienced ethnic growth. The Gospel was extended beyond the Jews to include Gentiles (people of all nations).

SPIRITUAL GROWTH:

Growth in numbers is not the only emphasis of spiritual multiplication. Converts must grow in spiritual quality as well as quantity, *"But grow in grace, and in the knowledge of our Lord and Savior Jesus Christ"* (2 Peter 3:18). *"...but, speaking the truth in love, may grow up in all things into Him who is head, even Christ..."* (Ephesians 4:15).

THE EMPHASIS ON NUMBERS

Some people ignore the subject of spiritual multiplication and church growth because they believe an emphasis on numbers is wrong, but in the Bible there are many records of God's concern with numbers. For examples, see Numbers 1:1-3; 2:23-24; 26:1-4; Revelation 7:9; 20:8; Genesis 22:17; and Hebrews 6:14.

Jesus told many parables concerning numeric growth. He also indicated that careful numeric records are kept in Heaven:

> *"I say to you that likewise there will be more joy in heaven over one sinner who repents than over ninety-nine just persons who need no repentance."*
> *(Luke 15:7).*

Multiplication is also emphasized in the record of the early Church (Acts 1:15; 2:41; 4:4; 6:7; 9:31; 12:24; 16:5; 19:20; and 28:30-31).

It is true that there can be an improper emphasis on numbers: when numerical growth becomes more important than spiritual growth or individuals; when it is motivated by pride; when ministry movements are judged by numbers; and when there is more emphasis on church growth than growth of the Kingdom at large.

Regardless of the potential of abuses, numbers are important to God. Jesus told His followers:

> *"Do you not say, 'There are still four months and then comes the harvest?' Behold, I say to you, lift*

up your eyes and look at the fields, for they are already white for harvest!" (John 4:35).

When God sends harvesters in to the spiritual fields of the world, He wants them to come back with sheaves, not excuses:

> *"Those who sow in tears shall reap in joy. He who continually goes forth weeping, bearing seed for sowing, shall doubtless come again with rejoicing, bringing his sheaves with him" (Psalms 126:5-6).*

THE PROCESS IN THE EARLY CHURCH

The following progression shows the initial states of multiplication resulting from Andrew, one of the first disciples of Jesus:

1. Andrew shared the Gospel with his brother, Peter.

2. Peter shared the Gospel on the day of Pentecost in Jerusalem.

3. Peter continues to share the Gospel with others who also become reproductive.

4. Thousands of believers scattered from Jerusalem continue to spread the Gospel.

5. Each person they reach becomes reproductive and the process continues.

The following diagram shows the first stages of spiritual multiplication resulting from Apostle Paul's ministry.

	Paul (S)	Timothy (S)	TOTAL
YEAR 5	103,680,000	X 12 =	1,244,160,000
YEAR 4	8,640,000	X 12 =	103,680,000
YEAR 3	720,000	X 12 =	8,640,000
YEAR 2	60,000	X 12 =	720,000
YEAR 1	5,000	X 12 =	60,000

1. Ananias is used of God to raise up Paul.
2. Paul disciples Timothy.
3. Paul continues on to disciple others.
4. Timothy disciples faithful men who can teach others.
5. Faithful men reach others.
6. These "others" continue the multiplication process.
7. Each person in the network continues to multiply.

GOD USES ORDINARY PEOPLE

The Bible tells little about the man named Ananias referred to in the above diagram. He was not known of man, but he was used of God to raise up the Apostle Paul. Andrew was a common, uneducated fisherman. But look at the chain of spiritual multiplication for which he was responsible!

You may not be well known by man. You may not be well known in your community or church denomination. You may be an ordinary person who works at ordinary tasks. But God can use you to multiply disciples through your commitment to The Mentor Center.

Read the story of the healing of the lame man in Acts 4. When Peter and John appeared before the council, it was obvious that they were uneducated, common men:

> *"Now when they saw the boldness of Peter and John, and perceived that they were uneducated and untrained men, they marveled; and they realized that they had been with Jesus. And seeing the man who had been healed standing with them, they could say nothing against it" (Acts 4:13-14).*

These common men had received new life through Jesus Christ and the life within them led to spiritual reproduction. Jesus entrusted the laity with the responsibility of spreading the Gospel. He took fishermen from their boats and made them into fishers of men. He believed that ordinary people could become extraordinary when empowered by the Holy Spirit.

Gideon was a farmer. Paul was a tentmaker. Moses was a shepherd. Luke was a doctor, and Joseph was a slave. Whatever your education or occupation, God can use you in His plan.

Where you are and who you are, is not important. It is what you are doing, where God has placed you. The key to effective spiritual multiplication is to be God's man or woman, in God's place, doing God's work, God's way. Get this deep into your spirit and transmit it to those you train.

Chapter 6

Mentoring Guidelines

This chapter provides guidelines for selecting and mentoring men and women to become servant leaders.

THE MENTORS

DEFINITION: The word "mentor" is defined as a trusted counselor and guide. As used in this manual, a mentor is one who guides another individual's development towards the specific goal of becoming equipped for Kingdom service.

WHAT A MENTOR DOES: A mentor selects and trains others for the work of the ministry and the extension of the Kingdom by:

- Transferring the DNA of the local church.
- Guiding students in completion of the core course training.
- Encouraging Godly behavior.
- Teaching biblical principles for an effective ministry.
- Dealing with negative behaviors or attitudes that might abort ministry.
- Providing experiences for spiritual growth and practical ministry.
- Leading by example as a positive role model.
- Offering wise counsel.
- Providing feedback.
- Serving as a resource for providing continuing training, prayer support, and networking.

MENTOR QUALIFICATIONS: What qualifies you to be a mentor?

- Your own spiritual experiences of new birth in Jesus Christ and infilling of the Holy Spirit.
- Familiarity with the ministry of Vision.
- Your own successful ministry experiences.
- A burning desire to communicate this vision and anointing to others.
- The best mentors are people whose own enthusiasm for ministry is so contagious that they inspire others just by doing what they enjoy most – sharing the Gospel of Jesus Christ in a demonstration of God's power.
- Minimal academic qualifications.

THE GOAL OF MENTORING: The goal of mentoring is to commit to faithful men and women the biblical revelations you have received through this ministry. As Paul commissioned Timothy,

> *"And the things that you have heard from me among many witnesses, commit these to faithful men who will be able to teach others also" (2 Timothy 2:2).*

We are training men and women to fulfill the Great Commission through dynamic, mature ministry:

> *Go therefore and make disciples of all the nations, baptizing them in the name of the Father and of the Son and of the Holy Spirit, teaching them to observe all things that I have commanded you; and lo, I am with you always, even to the end of the age. Amen. (Matthew 28:19-20)*

OUR MODEL FOR MENTORING: Our model for mentoring is the Lord Jesus Christ.

THE STUDENTS

DEFINITION: A "Timothy" is the name used for the students you train in The Mentor Center.

CHARACTERISTICS OF A POTENTIAL TIMOTHY:

- Born-again, Spirit-filled.
- Have a positive reputation.
- Recommended by a spiritual leader.
- Committed to the vision of the ministry.
- Able to work cooperatively with others.
- Willing to receive direction and correction.
- Commitment to extend The Mentor Center.
- Age 18 or older. (If under age 18, parental consent must be obtained.)

PRINCIPLES OF SELECTION

You are just one person with only so much available time, so you cannot train everyone. This means you must select those whom you will train. You could choose on the basis of education, experience, tests, or by trial and error. But the best way to select is to follow the biblical principles Jesus used in selecting His disciples. The record of His selection is given in Matthew 5:1; 10:2-4; Mark 3:13-19; Luke 6:12-16; and Luke 10:1-16. Here are some important principles Jesus followed which you should also use in selecting those who you will train:

DEPEND ON GOD: Jesus depended on God in everything He did, including the selection of those He would train in ministry. Jesus declared, *"I can of Myself do nothing. As I hear, I judge; and My judgment is righteous, because I do not seek My own will but the will of the Father who sent Me"* (John 5:30).

MAKE IT A MATTER OF PRAYER: Luke 6:12-13 records that Jesus spent the whole night in prayer before selecting His disciples. Pray for wisdom to select faithful men and women.

TAKE THE INTIATIVE: Jesus took the initiative to call His disciples. People will not flock to you to become part of The Mentor Center. You must take the initiative to call them.

LOOK AT POTENTIAL, NOT PROBLEMS: When Jesus selected disciples, He called common men. Some were uneducated and they all had faults and failures. It has been said that if the original 12 disciples were reviewed by a church mission board in the present time, they would be turned down for missionary service. But Jesus operated on the basis of potential, not problems. He did not choose men and women because of what they were, but because of what they could become. He looked beyond their problems to their potential.

MAKE THE SPIRITUAL COSTS CLEAR: When Jesus selected disciples, He made it clear what it would cost. They must forsake all (Luke 14:33). The Kingdom of God must become the main priority (Matthew 6:31-33). They must deny self by taking up the cross:

> *Then Jesus said to His disciples, "If anyone desires to come after Me, let him deny himself, and take up his cross, and follow Me" (Matthew 16:24).*

> *And whoever does not bear his cross and come after Me cannot be My disciple (Luke 14:27).*

SELECT MEN AND WOMEN WHO MEET BIBLICAL STANDARDS: These standards include:

- **Faithfulness:** Paul told Timothy to select faithful people and commit to them the things he had been taught. These faithful people were to have the ability to teach others. The basic requirements are faithfulness and the ability to teach others. If a person is not faithful, he will not fulfill his responsibility of spiritual reproduction. If he is faithful but does not know how to teach others, then he will also fail. Faithfulness involves spiritual maturity, but faithful men are not necessarily faultless men. They are believers who are in the process of developing Christ-like qualities in their lives. Even faithful men have problems and weaknesses to overcome, as did the original disciples. The world takes talented men and attempts to give them character. They focus on creating professionals. God said to take faithful men of character and He will empower them with spiritual talents and abilities.

- **Availability:** Select men and women who are available. When Jesus selected Simon and Andrew, they immediately left their nets. The word "immediately" reveals their availability. Those you select must be available and willing to make this vision the priority of their lives.
- **Spiritual Vision:** Faithful men and women are motivated by spiritual vision. When Jesus gave Peter and Andrew the vision of catching souls, it motivated them to leave their nets.
- **Hunger For The Word:** Faithful men and women have a hunger for the Word of God, as did Christ's disciples. Their hearts burned within them as He shared the Scriptures (Luke 24:32-45).
- **Love For God:** Faithful men and women are marked by a love for God and man. They take seriously the first and second greatest commands (Mark 12:30-31).
- **A Servant's Heart:** An Elisha must be willing to be a servant to all. (Matthew 10:25, 20:26-28).

PRINCIPLES OF MENTORING

After selecting His disciples, Jesus demonstrated eight important principles in mentoring them which are worthy of emulation.

1. **ASSOCIATION:** When Jesus called His disciples, He called them to be with Him. He shared His life intimately with His disciples. You cannot train people through committee meetings, Sunday worship services, or formal class sessions alone. There must be close association with

those whom you train. You must share your life with them. You must come to know them, their problems, and their spiritual issues.

2. **CONSECRATION:** Out of association with Jesus, consecration developed. Jesus called His disciples to consecrate to a person, not a denomination or organization, and He called for absolute obedience to His Word and His purposes (John 4:34; 5:30; 15:10; 17:4; and Luke 22:42). The obedience is to the Word of Jesus and His purposes, not obedience to you the Mentor leader.

3. **VISION:** Jesus motivated His followers by giving them spiritual vision. He called them to a task greater than the routine of everyday living. He called them to be fishers of men (Matthew 4:19). He gave them a vision of worldwide spiritual harvest (John 4:35). He challenged them with the revelation of the Kingdom of God (Matthew 13).
   Without vision, people perish (Proverbs 29:18). They have no direction and no motivation. As you train others, you must communicate spiritual vision to motivate the mission. The vision is worldwide conquest with the Gospel of the Kingdom. Never be distracted by a lesser cause.

4. **INSTRUCTION:** Jesus spent a great part of His time teaching his disciples. His instruction always related to the vision He had given them. If you are to train disciples following the methods of Jesus, then you must teach what Jesus taught. This is part of the command of the Great commission (Matthew 28:20). Through THE MANTLE mentoring materials that have been placed in your hands, you have a wealth of biblical teaching to share with your students.

5. **DEMONSTRATION:** Jesus did not teach through verbal instruction alone. He demonstrated what He taught. Jesus taught healing and demonstrated it by healing the sick. He taught the authority of the believer over Satan and demonstrated it by casting out demons. He taught concern for the poor and illustrated it by feeding the multitudes.

The disciples were not only students, they were eye witnesses to the demonstration of God's power. They later said they were teaching "that which we have seen and heard" (1 John 1:1). Jesus taught by example. He demonstrated what He said by how He lived and ministered. (John 13:15, Acts 8:6).

Paul spoke not only of the truth of the Gospel (Galatians 2:5) but of the power of the Gospel (Romans 1:16). He declared and demonstrated the Gospel (1 Corinthians 2:1, 4). Produce the proof, and your students will hear you.

6. **PARTICIPATION:** Mere knowledge is not enough. To be effective, knowledge must be applied. There comes a time for action. The disciples not only listened to the teachings of Jesus and observed the demonstrations of God's power, they also participated. Teaching a subject is not enough to assure learning. Teaching alone is like trying to learn to do surgery by reading a book. Your Timothies must actually experience what they are learning. They must gain experience in how to share the Gospel, how to pray for the sick, how to cast out demons, etc. Jesus provided such opportunities for His disciples. Read Mark 6:7-13 and Luke 9:1-6. Jesus sent His disciples out to experience what they had been taught.

7. **SUPERVISION:** When the disciples of Jesus returned from their ministry trip, Jesus evaluated their efforts (Luke 9:10). Throughout the entire training process Jesus supervised His disciples. They were not left alone in their struggles. He was there to correct, rebuke, and encourage them.

You cannot assume that the work will be done merely because you have shown a willing student how to do it and sent him out with glowing expectations. You must supervise. As the student faces frustration and obstacles, you must teach him how to meet these challenges. Paul did this as he returned to strengthen the churches he planted.

After he had spent some time there, he departed and went over the region of Galatia and Phrygia in order, strengthening all the disciples (Acts 18:23).

Strengthening the souls of the disciples, exhorting them to continue in the faith, and saying, "We must through many tribulations enter the kingdom of God" (Acts 14:22).

8. **DELEGATION:** The final stage of the discipleship process was when Jesus delegated His followers to become disciple-makers themselves. He gave them the task of spiritual multiplication throughout the nations of the world. You will delegate to your students a similar responsibility, that of reaching the world with the Gospel in a demonstration of power and authority. You will also delegate to them the challenge to raise up other anointed Timothies.

Chapter 7

The Importance of CURRICULUM

When you begin a mentoring center, you will need to have mentoring materials. There are many groups that offer curriculum to teach and mentor from, but of course, we recommend the conservative charismatic curriculum from Vision International University and the International Training College from our Ramona headquarters.

The core courses of a mentoring program consist of the basic curriculum developed by the Vision team, led by Dr. Ken Chant and Dr. Stan DeKoven, with a host of others, developed over the past 40 plus years.

MENTOR CENTER PHILOSOPHY

The Mentor Center is not a seminary for those who desire theological debate or training in biblical languages, archaeology, history, etc. The Mentoring Center curriculum is not for teaching denominational tenets, nor do we desire to create a denominational structure. We are working between denominations, churches, organizations, and nations to raise up a mighty army of spiritual Timothies.

The Mentoring Center is not a self-improvement program. God is not teaching self-improvement, but is taking dead men and women and making them spiritually alive. That is radically different from self-help.

The Mentoring Center takes training to believers' right in the context of their own culture, allowing their daily activities to remain stable while becoming a laboratory for application of what they are learning.

Thus, Vision does not spend millions of dollars on brick and mortar to build training centers. The Mentoring program can be offered in existing facilities, whether a home, church building, or school. Jesus did not construct buildings, yet he took men from vision to reality. It is the content, not the physical facility, which establishes spiritual reproduction.

The curriculum emphasizes demonstration, training laymen to be participators rather than spectators. Intellectual knowledge of God is not enough:

> *But be doers of the word, and not hearers only, deceiving yourselves (James 1:22).*

True knowledge is gained only by experience. Study results in gaining information, but not experience. Teaching is factual while training is experiential. Jesus is a living person, not merely a fact. Relationship to Him is based on experience, not just knowledge, facts, and information. The aim of the training is not accumulated knowledge, but action which converts the possibilities of ministry into reality. It is not just articulation (talking about the power of God), but demonstration (putting it into action).

> *And my speech and my preaching were not with persuasive words of human wisdom, but in demonstration of the Spirit and of power, that your faith should not be in the wisdom of men but in the power of God (1 Corinthians 2:4-5).*

All Mentoring Centers desire that men and women learn the truth, and learn to walk in the truth of God's word (Luke 1:4). The curriculum goes beyond teaching to training where participation is required. The participation to which students are challenged is that of spiritual reproduction, which was Christ's first appeal to His disciples (Matthew 4:19). His final command to them was the same: To reproduce spiritually.

> *Go therefore and make disciples of all the nations, baptizing them in the name of the Father and of the Son*

and of the Holy Spirit, teaching them to observe all things that I have commanded you; and lo, I am with you always, even to the end of the age. Amen (Matthew 28:19-20).

The Church is a spiritual body under commission. Since 99 percent of the Church is composed of laymen, this force must be motivated to become reproductive in order to harvest the spiritual fields of the nations of the world.

Through application of Scriptural principles, this training results in each believer having the potential to raise up other motivated Christians, creating a new network of evangelism throughout the world.

This is not a plan developed by an individual or an organization, but the plan of God revealed in Scriptures. It is based on the principle given by the Apostle Paul to a young minister named Timothy:

> *"And the things that you have heard from me among many witnesses, commit these to faithful men who will be able to teach others also" (2 Timothy 2:2).*

THE CORE COURSES

The following are recommended courses for a Mentoring Center, and are the core of the ITC Mentoring Center. Each course should include textbooks for personal study, audio-video teaching and a course syllabus which includes course objectives, notes, and a final examination.

Associate of Arts in Ministry (A.A.)

Year 1: Christian Ministry Education Focused on Discipleship

The standard first year (Year 1) of the Vision Undergraduate study program leading to the Associates' degree is focused on discipleship. Year One is an introductory level course of study, acclimating the student to core concepts of the four-year Bachelor's degree program. The first year consists of 10 subjects; upon completion, the student may proceed to Year 2.

- **BI 100** Hermeneutics: Introduction to Bible Study
  - **BI 201** The Gospel of John
  - **CC 101** Sociology of Marriage and Family Life
  - **GE 103** English Composition
  - **GE 112** Introduction to Management
  - **RS 101** Dynamic Christian Foundations
  - **RS 102** Christian Life
  - **RS 103** Intro to Communication: Evangelism
  - **RS 109** Spiritual Formation: Journey to Wholeness
  - **RS 219** Christian Character Development

Year 2: Christian Ministry Education Focused on Service

The standard second year (Year 2) of the Vision Undergraduate study program leading to the Associates' degree is focused on service. Year Two builds upon the Year One program. Year Two consists of 10 subjects; upon completion, the student may proceed to the Advanced Diploma of Christian Ministry.

- **BI 101** Old Testament Survey
  - **BI 103** The Pentateuch

- o **BI 202** The Book of Acts

- o **BI 203** Pauline Epistles: Romans

- o **CC 201** Intro to Psychology: Christian Counseling Perspectives

- o **ED 101** Dynamics of Teaching

- o **GE 220** Financial Integrity and Stewardship

- o **RS 105** Theology of Worship

- o **RS 209** Faith Dynamics

- o **RS 212** Speech and Communication: Homiletics

Christian Ministry Education focused on Leadership

Year Three Courses (Transitional Year): 30 Credit Hours of the Vision Undergraduate study program leading to the Bachelor's degree. The transitional year builds upon the Associate Degree and prepares the student to enter the Bachelor's program (Year 4). The transitional year consists of 10 subjects; upon successful completion, the student may proceed to the Bachelor's program.

- • **BI 302** Major and Minor Prophets of the Old Testament

  - o **CC 301** Self-Concept: Studies in Biblical Inner Healing

  - o **GE 201** Cultural Anthropology: A Christian Perspective

  - o **RS 200** History of Civilization I: Church History Perspectives

- RS 210 The Blood Covenant

- RS 217 Introduction to Charismatic Theology

- RS 301 Pastoral Ministry

- RS 304 Introduction to Leadership

- RS 305 Introduction to World Missions

- RS 314 Principles and Philosophy of Church Growth

Bachelor's Degree Program

One key to help in the marketing of a Mentor Program is to have the local church connected by articulation to a college or University that can provide bible degrees or diplomas for their students. One such institution is Vision International University.

Chapter 8

The School With A Difference

The Mentoring Center is committed to ministry training by making involvement in actual ministry a part of the overall program. By doing this, you will provide those you train with challenging opportunities to put into practice what they are learning. They will become participants instead of mere spectators. The hands-on involvement in the real-life laboratory of your church, ministry, community and nation makes The Mentoring Center become a "school with a difference."

GIFT-BASED MOBILIZATION

Gift-based mobilization is a method of commissioning those you train for practical ministry on the basis of their spiritual gifts, guiding them to do what God has called and equipped them to do. The goal is not just to fill vacant ministry positions or to get people involved. It is to prayerfully guide those you train into areas of service for which their spiritual gifts and experience best equip them. There are three major steps in gift-based mobilization:

1. Guide Timothies to discover their spiritual gifts.
2. Identify ministry needs.
3. Match Timothies with the proper gifts to the needs identified.

STEP ONE: Guide Timothies to Discover Their Spiritual Gifts.

Prayerfully guide each Timothy to identify their spiritual gifts. Spiritual gifts are itemized in the following passages: Romans 12:1-8, 1 Corinthians 12:1-31, Ephesians 4:1-16, and 1 Peter 4:7-11. Teach your Timothies about these gifts, then pray for the gifts to be manifested in their lives, and lay your hands on them to impart the anointing.

STEP TWO: Identify Ministry Needs.

What needs does your church have? Your community? What new ministries do you believe the Lord would have you doing for which you will need laborers? Here are some possible ministry needs:

Visitation: sick, newcomers to church, members of church, hospital, widows, prisons, bereaved, home for aged.

Evangelism: House-to-house, evangelistic services, crusades, open-air services.

Follow-Up Ministry: To new converts.

Office/administrative Support: Typing, drawing (art), filing, assembling, and reproducing materials, mailings, telephones, records.

Hospitality: Cooking meals and providing lodging for those in need or for visiting ministers, evangelists, etc.

Ministry to Poor: Providing food, clothing, and shelter.

Maintenance of Church Buildings: Landscaping, painting, carpentry, electrical, plumbing, cleaning.

Music: Choir, instruments, song leader, special music groups, soloist, writing music.

Drama: Religious Dramatic Productions.

Financial: Fund raising, accounting, financial planning for ministers.

Writing: Christian books, newsletters, tracts, news and magazine articles, poetry.

Multimedia: Audio and video tapes, CDs and DVDs, radio, television, satellite broadcasting, internet.

Counseling: General counseling or counseling to specific groups; telephone counseling.

Ministry to Special Groups: Deaf, blind, mentally ill, drug addicts, alcoholics, migrant workers, gangs, unwed mothers, homosexuals, Jews, minority groups, women, men, families, married couples, abused children, runaways, school dropouts, illiterate, prisoners, military, children, youth, aged and others.

Church Offices: Elder, deacon/deaconess, Sunday school teacher, usher, committees such as building, finance, etc.

Translation: Bible and Christian literature.

Christian Education: Sunday school, Vacation Bible School, Christian preschool, elementary, high school, college; training for laymen, establishing Schools of Ministry.

Missionary/Church Planting: To unreached peoples in your region/nation.

Literature: Christian library, bookstore, Bible and Christian literature distribution.

STEP THREE: Match Timothy's, Gifts, and Needs.

Now you are ready to match Timothies with the proper gifts to the ministry needs you have identified. Gift-based mobilization will not only provide practical experience, but will launch those you train into their specific realm of fruit-producing service in the Kingdom of God.

EVALUATION

You will know a Timothy is properly placed on the basis of gifts when:

1. He is fruitful in the area in which he is serving. You see positive results of his ministry.
2. When he is fulfilled and enjoying the ministry. If he is frustrated, he may be serving in an area for which he is not gifted.
3. When the feedback you receive from those to whom he ministers is positive, which indicates he is effective in the position in which he is serving.

THE MENTOR CENTER REPORTS

Each Mentor Center, if affiliated with a college or University, will be required to be accountable for students' records, etc. Thus, they must submit reports as required. However, since your purpose is not to be an institution, it would behoove you to seek out a relationship with a mentoring center program that minimizes your paperwork by its effective support services.

Conclusion

Every five fold ministry leader understands that their primary responsibility is to equip the saints for the work of ministry until they become fully mature in Christ. The process for making disciples is called mentoring, and requires teaching, training and activation. The ultimate goal is to help men and women to greater maturity, while assisting them to know Christ better, and become all he has already made them to be in him.

The process of mentoring men and women to maturity, and into some area of Christian service is noble, necessary and never easy. It takes dedication, a heart of love and patience, and a grace from the Lord. Discipleship through mentoring is really not an option; it is essential. The question is not shall we make disciples, but how do we do it in a most effective, Kingdom enhancing fashion. I pray for your every success as you engage in the teaching and training of the next generation of servant leaders for the glory of God.

Appendix

Affiliation with Vision International University as your Mentor Center

The Process

Affiliation with a College or University is important for additional support and greater credibility. The fact that you have purchased this book indicates your interest in developing a Mentor Center. Thus, we have provided here a simple process for you to move from interest to activation...and become a dynamic, life changing Mentoring Center for the Kingdom of God.

To be considered to direct a Mentor Center, an applicant must have:

- Completed a mentor training program in seminar, on or off line, or webinar AND must commit to continue the training of men and women via mentoring.
- All mentored students are students of International Training College or Vision International University. The student must complete applications and be formerly evaluated and accepted into our program prior to assignment to you as a mentoree.

THE MISSION STATEMENT

The mission of the Vision Mentoring Center is to:

- Transfer through distance education and personal mentoring the dynamic education to transform men and women into workers and servant leaders.
- Equip key leaders to train those who have the spiritual hunger, capability, and willingness to be used by God in the spiritual harvest fields of the world.

- Raise up men and women with the spiritual capabilities to be used by God in the supernatural, ordinary people who become extraordinary through the anointing of the Holy Spirit.
- Recruit a spiritual team whose members are capable of articulation of the Word of God and demonstration of the power of God.
- Redefine the meaning of the word "minister" to include all born-again believers ministering in their spheres of influence.
- Demonstrate to the world the five-fold ministries outlined in Ephesians 4:11-12 for the perfecting of the saints, the work of the ministry, and the edifying of the Body of Christ.
- Establish a network of trained Pauls and Timothies to overtake the lost in this generation and proclaim the Gospel to every nation.

The Application

Thus, to become a Vision-ITC Mentor Center, it is as easy as going to www.vision.edu.

About the Author
Dr. Stan DeKoven

Dr. Stan DeKoven is the International President of Vision International University[5], and founder/President of the International Training and Education Network[6]. Vision/ITEN specializes in establishing and supporting local, Church-based Bible Colleges and distance education programs. Through their unique "Bible College in a Box" system, they are presently serving more than 4,000 Resource Centers in over 150 countries and over 100,000 students through its affiliated ministries.

Stan has a diverse background in Education, Business, Military, Leadership and Counseling. He has pioneered two very successful businesses while consulting with others nationally and internationally. Stan has earned a Bachelors degree in Psychology from San Diego State University, a Masters degree in Counseling from Webster University, a Doctor of Ministry degree from Evangelical Theological Seminary and a Doctor of Philosophy in Counseling Psychology from the Professional School of Psychological Studies. Dr. DeKoven holds credentials in School Psychology, Marriage and Family Therapy, and clinical membership in many professional organizations. He specializes in Leadership development, and assisting executives achieve their potential in the marketplace. He is also an Executive Coaching

---

[5] Vision International University (www.vision.edu) is a California State Degree granting Institution, primarily offering their programs on line or by direct distance (correspondence) and Church based programs. Vision has offered Associate-Doctorate, in Theology, Leadership, Counseling and Christian Education since 1989.

[6] The International Training and Education Network offers practical training in religious studies through the International Training College in over 140 nations, and in multiple languages, publishes Christian literature in multiple languages, and certifies ministers and counselors for service in an through the local church.

Specialist for The Vision Group, and the founder of Walk in Wisdom media ministries.

He is a licensed Marriage and Family Therapist in the State of California with over 35 years of professional services, specializing in:

- Crisis Ministry
- Domestic Violence and Recovery
- Substance Abuse Treatment
- General Family problems with children and Teens.
- Personal Coaching for men and women seeking improvement in vocation or relationship.

Credentials:
President: Vision International Education Services, Inc., sponsor of Vision International University
President: International Training and Education Network, sponsors of Vision Publishing, Walk in Wisdom Ministries and Family Care Services.
Former Associate Pastor: Christian Life Center; Senior Pastor, Vision Christian Church International
Clinical Director: Restoration Ranch
Member: Who's Who California and Outstanding Men of America
Certified Life and Executive Coach with the Institute for Motivational Living
Clinical Member: California and American Association of Marriage and Family Therapists
Clinical Member: American Christian Counselor Association
Chairman: International Association of Christian Counseling Professionals.
Certified Member of the American Chaplains Association

BOOKS BY DR. DEKOVEN:

- Crisis Counseling

- Family Violence: Patterns of Destruction

- Substance Abuse Therapy

- Kingdom Quest: The Journey to Wholeness
  New Beginnings: A Sure Foundation
  Marriage and Family Life

- On Belay! An Introduction to Christian Counseling
  Group Dynamics
  I Want to Be Like You, Dad: Breaking Free and
  Discovering the Father's Heart
  Grief Relief

- Parenting on Purpose

- Old & New Testament Surveys

- Fresh Manna (How to Study The Bible)

- Leadership in the Church: In the Eye of the Storm

- Visionary Leadership

- Prelude to a Requiem: Principles of Leadership from the
  Upper Room

- Supernatural Architecture (The Apostolic Church of 21st
  Century & Beyond)

And 20+ more books and booklets in various topics, see at
www.booksbyvision.com

Dr. Stan speaks on a wide range of topics from Christian Business, Christian Counseling, Leadership, Team Dynamics, Personal Coaching, Church Consultancy, Setting up Local Church Counselling, Teaching and Mission Ministries, World & Urban

Missions, Youth, Church Structure and Personal and Corporate Vision.

Dr. Stan assists many younger ministers develop in ministry and through speaking and consulting, giving relational oversight to churches both nationally and internationally. As such, he is in demand around the globe to speak at Leadership Conferences and to teach in Bible Colleges/Universities.

To schedule speaking or contact the author:

Vision International University
www.vision.edu
Walk in Wisdom Ministries
www.drstandekoven.com

www.ingramcontent.com/pod-product-compliance
Lightning Source LLC
Chambersburg PA
CBHW062033040426
42447CB00010B/2267